PETITIONING THE
COURTS OF
HEAVEN
DURING A TIME OF
CRISIS

PRAYERS THAT GET HELP IN
TIMES OF TROUBLE

ROBERT
HENDERSON

DESTINY IMAGE® PUBLISHERS, INC.
PO Box 310, Shippensburg, PA 17257-0310
"Promoting Inspired Lives"

This book and all other Destiny Image and Destiny Image Fiction books are available at Christian bookstores and distributors worldwide.

For more information on foreign distributors, call 717-532-3040.

Or reach us on the Internet: www.destinyimage.com

ISBN 13 TP: 978-0-7684-5675-2

ISBN 13 eBook: 978-0-7684-5665-3

For Worldwide Distribution, Printed in the U.S.A.

1 2 3 4 5 6 / 23 22 21 2

CONTENTS

INTRODUCTION

The Court of Heaven has answers in times of trouble and crisis. When we know how to petition this realm, we can see what the Bible promises become a reality. Many have tried to pray but haven't seen the desired breakthrough and victory they desperately need. It would seem they have entered a time of crisis only to be denied from Heaven their passion and longings fulfilled. The Bible is filled with stories of people who entered times of crisis only to see the Lord deliver them from their enemies. The word *crisis* in Chinese actually means a *dangerous opportunity*. In every crisis there is an opportunity. This means we can come out in a different place than where we went in.

Crises are places where heroes are made. Crises are places where hidden ones are revealed—those who have always been there, people just didn't recognize them. Crisis properly handled can bring exaltation and promotion. Yet the ability to see this happen comes from knowing how to handle the crisis in prayer and before the Courts of Heaven. The devil desires to use the crisis to destroy; the Lord, however, would use it to unveil and redirect His people and even culture into destiny and purpose. For this to happen, God needs a proactive people to function before Him in the Courts of Heaven. These people all had one thing in common—they knew how to approach the throne of God, even the Courts of Heaven. We are told in Daniel 7:9-10 that there is a very real *Court* we can petition. Daniel, as a prophet of God, saw it.

I watched till thrones were put in place,

And the Ancient of Days was seated;

His garment was white as snow,

And the hair of His head was like pure wool.

His throne was a fiery flame,

Its wheels a burning fire;

A fiery stream issued

And came forth from before Him.

A thousand thousands ministered to Him;

Ten thousand times ten thousand stood before Him.

The court was seated,

And the books were opened.

Notice that there is much activity in this Court that we actually are allowed to approach. This is why Jesus in teaching on prayer pictured it as approaching a judge in Luke 18:1-8. In this story Jesus speaks of a widow seeking a verdict from an unjust and unrighteous judge. He refuses her several times but finally, because of her persistence, grants her request.

> *Then He spoke a parable to them, that men always ought to pray and not lose heart, saying: "There was in a certain city a judge who did not fear God nor regard man. Now there was a widow in that city; and she came to him, saying, 'Get justice for me from my adversary.' And he would not for a while; but afterward he said within*

himself, 'Though I do not fear God nor regard man, yet because this widow troubles me I will avenge her, lest by her continual coming she weary me.'"

Then the Lord said, "Hear what the unjust judge said. And shall God not avenge His own elect who cry out day and night to Him, though He bears long with them? I tell you that He will avenge them speedily. Nevertheless, when the Son of Man comes, will He really find faith on the earth?"

The main lesson Jesus was teaching in this parable was that if this woman who had no power, might, nor clout could get a verdict from an unjust judge, how much more can we see God the righteous judge move on our behalf. Jesus placed prayer in a judicial setting. This is the setting we can be stepping into when we, by faith, come before the Courts of Heaven. Isaiah 43:26 encourages us to come into this place as well.

Put Me in remembrance;

Let us contend together;

State your case, that you may be acquitted.

We are exhorted to call God to remembrance of His word, His promises, His prophetic things concerning us and any other thing He might have said. When we do this, we are presenting cases before the Court and asking to be justified and exonerated. We are petitioning the Courts of Heaven to move on our behalf and bring deliverance to us and our circumstances. One verdict from the Court of Heaven will shift things from crisis to comfort. It can take it from a place of perplexity to peace and defeat to dominion. We can see this in Daniel 7:25-27. Daniel saw that in dealing with the anti-Christ spirit that would seek to take over the world, it was activity in and from the Courts of Heaven that solved this dilemma. What a powerful understanding.

He shall speak pompous words against the Most High,

Shall persecute the saints of the Most High,

And shall intend to change times and law.

Then the saints shall be given into his hand

For a time and times and half a time.

But the court shall be seated,

And they shall take away his dominion,

To consume and destroy it forever.

Then the kingdom and dominion,

And the greatness of the kingdoms under the whole heaven,

Shall be given to the people, the saints of the Most High.

His kingdom is an everlasting kingdom,

And all dominions shall serve and obey Him.

The saints were in crisis. The devil and his anti-Christ agenda had them in a very precarious and fearful place. Notice the Bible says *"but."* The Court of Heaven and what it was about to do was the solution to the crisis that was in the earth and against God's people. They were in a place of defeat. However, with one verdict from the Courts of Heaven, dominion was given to them. The very people who were being ruled over and destroyed were then set in the place of authority, honor, and privilege. They moved from defeat to dominion

14

as a result of the operation of the Court of Heaven. The Court of Heaven is our answer in the times of crisis and trouble. We can see the passion of God move for us because we have learned how to traverse this dimension. The place of crisis can and will become the place of conquering.

Lord, in these times of pressure and stress, I thank You that there is grace to enter Your Courts. I ask the Courts of Heaven for decisions that will move me from crisis to conquering. I petition this Court that You would remember me and move on my behalf to see Your deliverance come. Thank You, Lord, for being my Savior, Deliverer, and Redeemer. In Jesus' Name, amen.

CHAPTER 1

CRUSHING SATAN

Times of trouble and tribulation touch all of us. It is an absolute of life. It doesn't matter how well we live life or *do* life. There will be places and moments of pain, fear, heartache, grief, and uncertainty. Jesus actually said this Himself in John 16:33.

These things I have spoken to you, that in Me you may have peace. In the world

> *you will have tribulation; but be of good cheer, I have overcome the world.*

The idea here is that even while we might be in tribulation, we can have peace. Our peace is not dependent on our circumstance. Our peace is dependent on our connection and union with Jesus. We are told in Philippians 4:6-7 that there is an indescribable and supernatural peace that can possess us in every trouble we might face.

> *Be anxious for nothing, but in everything by prayer and supplication, with thanksgiving, let your requests be made known to God; and the peace of God, which surpasses all understanding, will guard your hearts and minds through Christ Jesus.*

Peace is a result of tapping the presence and closeness of the Lord through prayer. We are told we are not to be worried or anxious about anything. Wow! What a statement. This would seem like an impossibility. When the storms of life are whirling about and trauma and drama are encircling our life, how can we not worry? Yet we are told there is a place where this can be experienced. This peace is something that *surpasses our understanding.* In other words, it isn't natural or normal. It is Heaven sent and experienced. Even we ourselves can't explain it, yet there is this calm and assurance in the midst of crisis that things are good and will end up well. Only the Lord can bring this to us.

When I have experienced this peace, sometimes I am tempted to think I am in denial. You know what that is. When things are bad and terrible in the natural yet they seem to be having no effect on you. Sometimes people are detached from reality and aren't facing what is upon them. However, at other times we are living under the awesome peace and confidence of God. We are certain that things are good, because the Holy Spirit in us is testifying to this fact. This word *guard* is the Greek word *phroureo*. It means to be a *watcher in advance, to mount guards as a sentinel.* This means that when this supernatural peace is in our lives in crisis and turmoil it is God letting us know that what is coming is good. We don't have to believe what the circumstance seems to be saying. We can believe what the Spirit of God is testifying to us instead.

The peace we have is the watcher looking down the road reporting that what is heading toward us is good. We have to learn how to trust the voice of *God's senti-nel and watcher* and the report it is bringing. This will allow us to embrace and enjoy the peace of God in the midst even of immense trouble. Notice that this peace is a result of prayer. It is a certain kind of praying, however. We are told that through *prayer, supplication, thanksgiving, and request,* this peace comes. These are four differ-ent expressions of petitioning God that do overlap with each other, but are none-theless individualistic in their nature. We will get into these kinds of praying before the Courts of Heaven. This will allow the peace of God to come into our life. This is absolutely necessary if we are to maneu-ver through crisis and trouble. Paul gave us a needed insight in Romans 16:20. We are told that Satan will be bruised and literally crushed under *our feet.*

And the God of peace will crush Satan under your feet shortly. The grace of our Lord Jesus Christ be with you. Amen.

Notice that it is the *God of peace* who will cause satan to be annihilated and his powers broken against us. The word *crush* is the Greek word *suntribo*. It means to *crush completely, to shatter, to break in pieces*. It comes from the Greek word *tribo*, which means *a rut or a worn track*. This means that the way satan is crushed is through a progressive and persistent activity in the spirit realm from peace. In other words, as we in patient continuance release our spiritual authority from the peace of God in us, we are wearing down and destroying the activities of satan against us. We are shifting things that would be allowing the crisis to occur. As we from peace set in place the authority of God, satan is crushed under our feet.

He is shattered and his works are broken to pieces. The answer to getting out of crisis is to defeat and destroy the one who is driving it. This would be satan. It is, however, the *God of peace* who will use our feet to do the crushing.

Please take notice that the crushing and destroying of the satanic powers is from a place of peace. The God of peace living on the inside of us accomplishes this through us. Everything we do must be from this position of peace. It is the feet filled with peace that crush satan and his intents. Satan knows this. So one of his chief goals is to remove us from the posture of peace. If he can bring calamity, trouble, crisis, and anguish to us and get us out of peace, then he wins. He has removed from us the feet that should be used to crush him. We must be in peace to crush his head with our feet.

This is why these four distinct kinds of praying are so important. It brings us into the *peace that surpasses understanding* and positions us in a place of functional authority over the devil and his forces. We then win! We are able to dismantle the spiritual forces driving any and all crises. We are able to see peace and tranquility return, because the peace in our heart gained and exercised through prayer has won the victories.

Lord, as I approach Your Courts, would You allow Your peace to possess my innermost being. Even in places of crisis, Lord, I thank You that You have overcome. I receive Your peace that allows me to see satan crushed under my feet. I ask that this crisis that he has brought would be solved and Your vindication of me would now be revealed. In Jesus' Name, amen.

CHAPTER 2

THE PLACE OF PRAYER

When we examine the four realms of prayer that bring peace and defeat anxiety, we see the first word used is *prayer* itself. Again, Philippians 4:6 emphasizes this idea.

> *Be anxious for nothing, but in everything by prayer and supplication, with thanksgiving, let your requests be made known to God.*

This word for prayer in the Greek is the word *proseuche*. It means prayer addressed to God and a place set apart that is suitable for prayer. There is something to be said for a trysting place. A *tryst* is defined as the action or practice of meeting a lover in private. This is why a place of prayer can be so powerful. The place we habitually pray in can become filled and saturated with the presence of God. This presence can welcome us every time we enter it. At the risk of being called religious, these dedicated places can be very special. Whatever a place is used for will welcome and contain the spirits associated with that activity. For instance, my wife Mary and I moved into a new home. We wondered if the office furniture I had would fit into the new space that would be my office in our new house. As we discussed this, I made the suggestion that perhaps we should buy new furniture to fit the new office. I could tell that Mary was reluctant concerning this. This somewhat puzzled me, because I was actually offering to buy new stuff, which she had never turned down before.

Finally, after several conversations about the office and if our present furniture would work and fit, she informed me that she didn't want to get new furniture. She wanted to keep the old. She then explained to me why. For 10-plus years I have traveled a lot. Sometimes as much as 240 days out of the year. Mary explained to me that when I would be gone, she would go and sit in my office. She said as she sat in my office she would sense the presence of God and even my presence that had saturated the furniture through the years of praying that had been done in that setting. She told me she could feel the Lord's closeness there as well as my spirit in that place. It ministered to her just because of what inhabited the place. She had concluded that the furniture as a part of my office was holding the very presence of the Lord. This is not farfetched. In fact, the Bible clearly alludes to this. For instance, we see the clothes of Jesus carrying the anointing because of the anointing that was on Him. When the woman with the issue of blood reached out and touched His clothes in Matthew 9:20-22, she was made completely whole.

> *And suddenly, a woman who had a flow of blood for twelve years came from behind and touched the hem of His garment. For she said to herself, "If only I may touch His garment, I shall be made well." But Jesus turned around, and when He saw her He said, "Be of good cheer, daughter; your faith has*

*made you well." And the woman was
made well from that hour.*

She didn't touch *Him*, she touched *His
clothes*. Jesus' clothes had become saturated
with the anointing that was on His life.
This is because the anointing is a substance
and is transferable. It will saturate that
which it is habitually exposed to. This is
why the *handkerchiefs* of Paul healed people
and caused demons to flee in Acts 19:11-
12. When these pieces of cloth touched the
demonized and those sick, they were deliv-
ered and healed.

> *Now God worked unusual miracles
> by the hands of Paul, so that even
> handkerchiefs or aprons were brought
> from his body to the sick, and the diseases
> left them and the evil spirits went out
> of them.*

There wasn't anything magical about these items; it was simply that they had become saturated with the very presence and anointing of God that was on Paul's life. The word *handkerchief* in the Greek is *soudarion*. It means *a towel for wiping the face of perspiration*. Paul, as a tent maker, would physically labor and sweat. These *handkerchiefs* were the rags he used to wipe the perspiration from himself. This may sound gross and even unsanitary. Yet God used these rags to carry the anointing of God. The perspiration that flowed from the pores of Paul's body also carried the anointing of God. These rags became *storage batteries* for the anointing and glory of God that was upon Paul.

You have a battery on your car that stores electricity. When you want to, you can turn the switch and the electricity will cause the car to start. The battery isn't generating the power; it is simply storing it. This is what Paul's handkerchiefs and aprons were doing. My point to all this is, it is possible for a physical place and even an item to carry the presence of God. When something has been dedicated to the Lord, God will anoint it.

When I led a local work we prayed every morning in a particular room of the church. Upward of perhaps twenty-five people would gather four days a week for usually at least two hours of prayer. We would worship, pray, and entertain the very presence of the Lord. There was a mat that was on the floor next to a door that exited outside. Just because of where we were in the room, I usually stood on that mat as I led this intense prayer time. One day during prayer, I stepped off the mat to pray for someone. One of my associates stepped on the mat as we were all just moving around. He told me as he stepped on the mat that the presence of God came over him. He said he thought it was his imagination, so he stepped off the mat and the sense of the presence left. He then stepped back on the mat and to his surprise it came over him again. He then realized that all the hours I had prayed standing on that mat had allowed the anointing of God to saturate it. The anointing and presence of God is tangible, transferrable, and a very real substance. When we dedicate a given location to the Lord for prayer as our trysting place, the place we meet our lover, that spot can become filled with God. The more worship, adoration, prayer, and communion with the Lord that occurs there, the more God's presence will inhabit it.

With that said, we should realize that just spending time with the Lord is one of the main purposes in prayer. This is one of the man agendas people miss in regard to the Court of Heaven. They want to learn principles and even formulas, but they don't open the time with Him. This will short-circuit the power we can find in the Courts of Heaven. In Luke 18:6-8 we see Jesus speaking of this need to spend time with the Lord and develop a history with God. This is critical to finding success in the Courts of Heaven.

> Then the Lord said, "Hear what the unjust judge said. And shall God not avenge His own elect who cry out day and night to Him, though He bears long with them? I tell you that He will avenge them speedily. Nevertheless,

when the Son of Man comes, will He really find faith on the earth?"

Jesus, in making the point about God giving justice to His elect or those who belong to Him, pointed out that those who have cried out day and night will be avenged speedily. Initially these verses confused me. It appeared to be saying two different things. On one hand Jesus was saying we must cry out day and night, implying a long, persistent time of prayer. However, He then says that the answer would come speedily in a verdict rendered on our behalf. As I considered and meditated I felt the Lord say to me, "Those who have a history with Me in prayer, who have spent the time, paid the price, and know My presence, when they step into My judicial system will receive quick and speedy decisions on their behalf." I have found this to be true. The time we spend in His presence will speak and give us status before Him in His Courts. The sacrifices made and the faith we operate in cause us to have a good report before Him. This is what is declared in Hebrews 11:39. Those who made sacrifices and stood in faith are before Him with a good report.

> *And all these, having obtained a good testimony through faith, did not receive the promise.*

This is speaking of all these mentioned in Hebrews 11. They are still waiting on the fullness of the promise to be possessed. However, they have a good testimony before God. This means they have a status in Heaven. We too can have a status in the heavenly realm before God. We do not have to die to have that. Enoch, before his translation, had this testimony that he pleased God according to Hebrews 11:5.

> *By faith Enoch was taken away so that he did not see death, "and was not found, because God had taken him"; for before he was taken he had this testimony, that he pleased God.*

The testimony or status Enoch has now in Heaven he had before in the earth. We don't have to die to be esteemed by Heaven. We can step into this place now as the history we have with God speaks on our behalf! This will cause speedy results to come from the Courts of Heaven. I asked someone who had an awareness of the Courts of Heaven why I had gotten such quick results while others didn't seem to. Without hesitation, they said it was because I had done the work. I had spent years in the presence of the Lord repenting and humbling myself before the Lord. Therefore, when I came before the Courts of Heaven and made my case, God was able to avenge me speedily.

Please do not let this discourage you if you haven't done what I am describing. Start now. If I had understood this, I am sure I could have gotten some breakthrough years ago. I wouldn't have had to wait. God is gracious and merciful and will move on your behalf as you set your heart toward Him. He loves you dearly and will answer your cry.

When Jesus chose His disciples, His first commission for them was just to be with Him. Mark 3:13-14 tells us of Jesus choosing those who would be the twelve disciples and later apostles.

And He went up on the mountain and called to Him those He Himself wanted. And they came to Him. Then He appointed twelve, that they might be with Him and that He might send them out to preach.

Jesus chose who He wanted to *be with Him*. Everything else they were to do would flow out of them simply spending time with Jesus. Allowing His life to saturate and fashion them as they enjoyed His presence was of utmost importance. Nothing can or will take the place of this. This is the purpose of prayer and having a dedicated place to seek the face of the Lord. God told Moses to do the same thing. Exodus 24:12 shows God commanding Moses to come up into the mountain, be separated to Him, and *be there*.

Then the Lord said to Moses, "Come up to Me on the mountain and be there; and I will give you tablets of stone, and the law and commandments which I have written, that you may teach them."

There are times when we need to just come apart to the Lord and *be there*. This is what Moses did at the command of the Lord. Exodus 24:15-16 tells us that Moses was just *there* for six days and on the seventh, God spoke to him. Six full days of just being with the Lord.

Then Moses went up into the mountain, and a cloud covered the mountain.

Now the glory of the Lord rested on Mount Sinai, and the cloud covered it six days. And on the seventh day He called to Moses out of the midst of the cloud.

Moses was in the glory of the Lord for these six days. He and God were communing together as the cloud of His presence rested on the mountain. The glory of who God is was revealed to Moses. From this place God called to Moses and began to give him the mandate. We can never sacrifice or eliminate this element of the journey. Spending intimate time with the Lord in the place of prayer is non-negotiable. This is essential to us standing in the Courts of Heaven, in the place of peace, and seeing satan crushed and crisis ended.

Do you have a trysting place with God? Is there a dedicated spot where you go to meet the One you love? If not, may the Lord help us to find such a place where we can commune with the Lord. Where He can reveal His heart to us as we open our heart to Him. Where we are fashioned into His image from glory to glory even as in the presence of the Lord.

As I approach Your Courts, Lord, I ask that You would grace me to just be with You. Even as You called Your earliest disciples to spend undistracted time, allow me, Lord, that place. I ask that I might bring my prayers before You habitually, even in a dedicated place both in the natural and the spiritual realm. Allow this history I develop with You to give me status in Your Courts that decisions would be rendered on my behalf. Let every crisis pass, Lord. Allow Your sovereign will to be done in my life. In Jesus' Name, amen.

Chapter 3

Bound in Prayer

As we seek to see satan crushed under the weight of God's peace in the Courts of Heaven, we must learn the power of persistent prayer. So often people are looking for a quick fix. However, nothing will replace persistent, faith-filled praying in the Courts of Heaven. Again, this is what we see in Philippians 4:6.

Be anxious for nothing, but in everything by prayer and supplication, with thanksgiving, let your requests be made known to God.

The word *supplication* is the Greek word *deesis*. It means a *prayer of supplication*. It comes from the word *deomai*. It means *a petition, to bind oneself.* This is the idea of joining yourself to a cry until what is being cried for is done. It's is the concept of fervent and fiery prayer with a passion that simply will not let go! Psalms 118:27 speaks of binding the sacrifice to the horns of the altar.

God is the Lord,

And He has given us light;

Bind the sacrifice with cords to the horns of the altar.

44

This is the picture of an animal that was a sacrifice being tied to the altar so that it couldn't get away as it was being sacrificed. As gruesome as this might sound in our culture, it does give us a thought concerning our commitment to prayer. Even though we wouldn't be so inhumane as to kill an innocent animal today on an altar, we are to present ourselves as living sacrifices before the Lord. Romans 12:1 gives us the illustration of us being a sacrifice offered to the Lord.

> *I beseech you therefore, brethren, by the mercies of God, that you present your bodies a living sacrifice, holy, acceptable to God, which is your reasonable service.*

We are to present ourselves as living sacrifices to God. The Lord is not wanting something dead. He desires that which is alive and living for Him. Even though our desire might be to serve the Lord fully and with complete sacrifice, we too need to be bound to the altar we are being sacrificed on as living sacrifices. The reason for this is in times of weakness, pain, and suffering, we would try to crawl off the altar. Therefore, we need to be bound as the sacrifice to that which we are being offered on.

This is especially true in regard to prayer. The altar of prayer is something we can easily be removed from. Therefore, there is a binding to it that is necessary. There can be several things that can cause us as living sacrifices to crawl off the altar if we aren't bound to it. One of the main things is distraction. Life is full of voices beckoning us to their interests. If there is not a full commitment and a binding to the altar of prayer, this will cause us to cease to be that

sacrifice. The fact is that the Lord desires
and demands that He be first in our lives.
When we allow distractions to remove us
from the altar of prayer, we are putting
other things before Him. This is one of the
reasons why early morning prayer is such a
strategic thing. When you do something
first thing in the morning, nothing else can
get in the way of it. David in Psalms 5:3
spoke of this.

> *My voice You shall hear in the morning,
> O Lord;*
>
> *In the morning I will direct it to You,*
>
> *And I will look up.*

The word *morning* in the Hebrew is *boqer*.
It means *dawn or breaking of day*. David is
proclaiming to the Lord a commitment to
seek Him first thing in the morning. At the
breaking of the day he would cry out to the

Lord. Psalms 119:147 also shows David calling to the Lord early in the morning.

I rise before the dawning of the morning,

And cry for help;

I hope in Your word.

As a result of David's hope and confidence in the word of God, it moved him to seek the Lord early. When we do this, it removes the distractions of the day and puts God first. Martin Luther the great reformer is said to have prayed three hours a day. John Wesley was known to pray four hours a day and in his later days to spend as much as eight hours a day in prayer. He is supposed to have said that, *"he thought very little of a man who did not pray four hours every day."* Suzanne Wesley, the mother of John Wesley, would pray for two hours almost every day with her apron pulled over her head as her ten children played around her. Such was her commitment to prayer. There are many, many other examples of prayer and the extravagant means people used to not be distracted from their devotion. If we are to be bound to prayer, we must battle with all diligence this enemy called distraction. We must set ourselves apart even in a militant way and refuse to allow compromise of that time.

Another thing that can cause us to remove ourselves from being bound to the altar of prayer is carnality. Carnality is not necessarily sin but simply allowing the natural to rule our lives rather than the spiritual. Carnal means that which is of the flesh. It is that which is of the natural and seen realm. This is why Paul encourages us in Colossians 3:1-2 to set our minds on the heavenly things above.

*If then you were raised with Christ,
seek those things which are above, where
Christ is, sitting at the right hand of
God. Set your mind on things above,
not on things on the earth.*

He is challenging us to not be carnal but
to be spiritual. If we let our minds dwell
only on the natural realm of the earth it will
steal away our passion to pray. However, if
we set our minds on spiritual issues, there
will be motivation and a longing to seek the
face of God. Whatever we give ourselves to
in our interests and our mind is what will
captivate us. We must allow the Holy Spirit
to stir us with the passion of God. That we
will long for what He Himself longs for.

If we are truly born again then we have
been raised with Christ. When Jesus died,
He didn't just die for us. We actually died

with Him. This means my desire for sin was put to death when He died. However, we also were raised with Him. This means that within us are desires for that which is heavenly, godly, and holy. Paul is declaring that we should stir those desires up and step out of carnality and into spirituality. Whether someone realizes it or not, if you belong to Jesus, there is within you a desire for heavenly things. Paul is telling us to turn our hearts and minds toward those things and begin to seek after them. When we do, we will be amazed that there is that within us that longs for the spiritual.

Another thing that can remove us from being bound to the altar as a sacrifice in prayer is worry and anxiety. This happened to Martha in Luke 10:40-42. Martha is troubled with serving. Mary, her sister, will not help her because she is sitting at the feet of Jesus. Martha approaches the Lord in her frustrations and levels her complaint.

> *But Martha was distracted with much serving, and she approached Him and said, "Lord, do You not care that my sister has left me to serve alone? Therefore tell her to help me."*

> *And Jesus answered and said to her, "Martha, Martha, you are worried and troubled about many things. But one thing is needed, and Mary has chosen that good part, which will not be taken away from her."*

Martha's had a problem. She couldn't see what was of the utmost purpose in the moment. It wasn't that what needed to be done in the natural wasn't important. It just wasn't the most important in this moment of time. This is where worry and anxiety can come from at times. We aren't able to discern what should be priority in a given time. Therefore, we don't know how to lay something aside temporarily to engage and focus on what should be of utmost priority now. This can cause a conflict in our soul. This can result in an upheaval that frustrates us and others around us. This worry, concern, and anxiety in Martha caused her not to be bound to the altar of prayer. We must know how to grab our minds and still them before the Lord. This can happen as we enter His presence. There is a place where we can be still and *know* He is God, even as Psalms 46:10 declares.

Be still, and know that I am God;

I will be exalted among the nations,

I will be exalted in the earth!

The Lord will show who He is. He doesn't even need our help. He just says be still, focus on Me, and watch things be subdued into divine order. He is the Master of every storm. Martha had yet to realize this. Therefore, she was given to anxiety and worry that untied her from the altar of the sacrifice of herself in prayer. Distractions, carnality, and worry can be used to remove us from the altar we are to be bound to. However, as we stay bound in prayer to that which we are called to touch in the spirit word, we will see great results. Our persistence in prayer will speak for us in the Courts of Heaven. It will be evidence before the Lord of our cry and passion and cause Him to remember us. This is what we need before His Courts. We need to be *remembered*. All these forms of prayer that produce the surpassing peace that allows us to crush satan speak in Heaven for us.

There are many scriptures that speak of this. They can bring us into remembrance before the Lord. Rachel understood this principle. Genesis 30:6 shows Rachel being aware that God has heard her voice.

> *Then Rachel said, "God has judged my case; and He has also heard my voice and given me a son." Therefore she called his name Dan.*

As a result of God hearing her voice and judging her case, a son was born. God remembering her is later assigned as the reason for other children being born. Genesis 30:22 clearly connects this.

> *Then God remembered Rachel, and God listened to her and opened her womb.*

The judge listened, heard her, and remembered her. If we are to have the judge remember us and render decisions on our behalf, we must have that which is speaking on our behalf. These kinds of prayer do that. Heaven is aware and these things are speaking to bring God into remembrance of us and our cry.

> *Lord, I ask that my supplication before You would be remembered. Forgive me for any time I have through distraction, carnality, and/or worry not been bound on the altar of prayer. Lord, I bind myself to my cry until You as judge remember me and move on my behalf. Let my prayers and cries speak before You and decisions be rendered now, in Jesus' Name, amen.*

CHAPTER 4

THANKSGIVING AND THE LORD'S SUPPER

As we seek to present our cry before the Courts of Heaven and be heard, the next thing mentioned in Philippians 4:6 is *thanksgiving*.

> *Be anxious for nothing, but in everything by prayer and supplication, with thanksgiving, let your requests be made known to God.*

This word *thanksgiving* in the Greek is *eucharistia*. It means a *grateful language to God*. In other words, not just an act of gratefulness, but a spirit of it that is possessing our lives. That we are approaching God through a spirit of thanksgiving and worship. We are not bitter, angry, and internally mad at God. We are adoring and worshiping Him for His goodness, even in hardship, calamity, and crisis. This grasps the attention of the Lord. This is why we are told to be *thankful in all things*. I Thessalonians 5:18 tells us this.

> *In everything give thanks; for this is the will of God in Christ Jesus for you.*

Giving thanks *in* all things speaks of having a heart of worship and adoration no matter what we are going through. No matter the crisis, we are worshiping God through it. Even in places of hardship and uncertainty, we focus on the Lord through our worship, believing He is working for us even if we can't see it. Our love for the Lord motivates us to do this. We are told this is the will of God for us. We never have to question if this is something we are to do. It is spelled out for us. The greater challenge is to actually do it. Whatever prayers we are offering to the Lord must be laced with thanksgiving. We can potentially see this with Martha and Mary when Lazarus died. As Jesus purposely delays His arrival, Lazarus dies from his affliction. Jesus arrives too late to help it would seem. Martha is the first to see Him and confronts Him in John 11:20-21.

> *Then Martha, as soon as she heard that Jesus was coming, went and met Him, but Mary was sitting in the house. Now*

Martha said to Jesus, "Lord, if You had been here, my brother would not have died."

Mary will later see Jesus and says the same exact words to Jesus as Martha has said. John 11:32 records these words.

Then, when Mary came where Jesus was, and saw Him, she fell down at His feet, saying to Him, "Lord, if You had been here, my brother would not have died."

Even though the words were exactly the same, they were from a different spirit. Martha's words were probably more about accusation. *If You had been here...* In other words, *"Where were You?"* Remember, Martha has a propensity to accuse others of not caring. She even did this in a very inferior situation. She accused Mary before Jesus of not helping and that Jesus didn't care (see Luke 10:40-42). She is probably angry and hurt that Jesus didn't get to them soon enough. She is implying they obviously are not *that* important to Him, that He would allow her brother to die. Mary, on the other hand, says the same words, but from a different spirit. You can see this because she fell at His feet in worship. Her words were not accusations, but they were worshipful. They were a statement of faith. *"Lord, if You had been here, my brother wouldn't have died. You are powerful and wonderful. Things would've been different. I worship You for who You are."* This was a thankful heart speaking to the Lord.

Our prayers must be laced with this kind of spirit. This aroma attached to our prayers will grab the attention of the Lord in His

Holy Court. This is the aroma filled with thanksgiving and adoration. We want to make sure that that which we are offering before the Lord has this pleasant aroma attached to it. Philippians 4:18 shows the apostle Paul commending the Philippian church for their offering.

> *Indeed I have all and abound. I am full, having received from Epaphroditus the things sent from you, a sweet-smelling aroma, an acceptable sacrifice, well pleasing to God.*

Their offering had an aroma that Paul said satisfied and moved the heart of God. Every *offering* we bring should have this kind of pleasant, sweet-smelling aroma that pleases God. Whether it is our literal offering, service, and/or prayers, our ambition should be to satisfy and bless the heart of God. This will cause us to be heard.

As we saw, the word for *thanksgiving* is *eucharistia*. Of course, this is where our English word *eucharist* comes from, which is about the Lord's Supper or communion. The term *eucharist* began to be used in the first or second century by Christians to describe the Lord's Supper. It was meant to reflect the thankfulness associated with adoring Jesus and what He did for us on the cross. When we speak of praying with thanksgiving it can be associated with the Eucharist/Lord's Supper. The life-giving ritual of the Lord's Supper can be incorporated into our prayer life. It seems that the early church partook of the Lord's Supper on a regular basis. Acts 20:7 says the church came together to break bread. This implies this was the purpose of their gathering.

Now on the first day of the week, when the disciples came together to break bread, Paul, ready to depart the next day, spoke to them and continued his message until midnight.

If this is a reference to communion, which it seems to be, then the administering of the Lord's Supper wasn't just a part of their gathering, it was the central part. They understood the power of partaking of the Lord's body and blood and rediscovering on a regular basis the power associated with covenant. The early church regularly practiced from a thankful heart the celebration and remembering of the covenant Jesus made with us through His body and blood. We are told that every time we partake of the Lord's Supper we proclaim His death until He comes in I Corinthians 11:26.

For as often as you eat this bread and drink this cup, you proclaim the Lord's death till He comes.

Through proclaiming the Lord's death, we are acknowledging all that He did for us. Our salvation, forgiveness, healing, breaking of curses, and all other needs are met through His death. When we partake, we are eating and drinking His life to ourselves. However, we are also prophetically declaring His coming. We are proclaiming that He is alive and will come again as the reigning King of Heaven and earth. We are proclaiming that we are His people in covenant with Him. All of this speaks before Heaven and causes us to be remembered. As we worship, adore, and thank Him, we are releasing an aroma that touches the heart of God even as it did in Noah's day. Genesis 8:20-22 proclaims that the worship of Noah through His offering was such a powerful aroma that God in response lifted the curse and reset things into order.

> *Then Noah built an altar to the Lord, and took of every clean animal and of every clean bird, and offered burnt offerings on the altar. And the Lord smelled a soothing aroma. Then the Lord said in His heart, "I will never again curse the ground for man's sake, although the imagination of man's heart is evil from his youth; nor will I again destroy every living thing as I have done.*
>
> *"While the earth remains,*
>
> *Seedtime and harvest,*
>
> *Cold and heat,*
>
> *Winter and summer,*

And day and night

Shall not cease."

Such is the power of a thankful heart before the Lord. May we progressively learn how to bring our prayers before the Lord in crisis and see the passion of God stirred. He will remember us and we will be saved.

> *As we approach Your Courts, O Lord, we come with a heart of thanksgiving. We lay aside every fear, unbelief, anger, and doubt and worship You as the Great I Am. We celebrate who You are, Lord Jesus, and Your offering on our behalf. We thank You for being the Lamb of God who was slain. Through communion we receive and remember who You are and celebrate what You have done. May this speak before Your Courts and cause us to be remembered*

before You. May the offering of my heart be pleasing before You. In Jesus' Name, amen.

CHAPTER 5

ASKING OF THE LORD

If the Lord is to hear us, then we must learn to ask of Him once things are speaking on our behalf before His Courts. The prayers, supplication, and thanksgiving are all powerful in their own right. However, making a request is very necessary. Once again, Philippians 4:6 tells us this is the final part of securing peace that can crush satan and end crisis times.

Be anxious for nothing, but in everything by prayer and supplication, with thanksgiving, let your requests be made known to God.

We are told that God knows what we have need of before we ask. Matthew 6:8 tells us that God is aware of our condition and needs.

Therefore do not be like them. For your Father knows the things you have need of before you ask Him.

The question would be then, "Why do we need to ask, if our loving Father already knows?" After all, we are told to *"let our request be known."* Even though God knows, we have to present it before Him. We must think of it as in a court scenario. A judge may know exactly what the party desires him to do, but he can't do it unless evidence is presented that will support it and an official request is made. Without this, even though the judge knows what is desired, he can't render a judgment on the party's behalf.

As I was teaching on the Courts of Heaven, a man who worked in a court system as a translator told me this story. A young attorney was seeking to make his case before a judge. As this young attorney went on and on, the judge patiently listened. As it continued, however, the judge finally stopped the young attorney. He said to him, "Young man, I know what you are trying to do, but you're going to have to give me a reason." The judge was saying, "I know the verdict you want, I'm even in agreement and want to give it to you, but you haven't given me the evidence I need to grant it." This is why we must *make our request known to God, even though He knows before we ask.*

We are in a judicial setting in the spirit world. We must know how to make our case, call God into remembrance, and see Him render a decision for us. We can do this through our prayers, supplications, thanksgiving, and then making known our request. One of my children found themselves in a natural judicial case. The lawyer they hired sent the paper work to them that would be presented to the judge overseeing the courtroom setting. My child then sent it to me. As I looked over it, I was amazed. There were many different paragraphs that stated, *"Whereas."* After each *whereas*, there was a statement of evidence presented. There were quite a few of these official presentations before the judge of evidence and testimony. At the end of all this was something called a *prayer*. It was what the attorney was asking the judge for based on the evidence just presented.

Even in a natural judicial system, the request made before the judge was called a *prayer*. This is exactly what we do before the Court of Heaven. We present our case before the Lord. Through *prayers,* we come before the Lord and love Him and are loved by Him. We allow Him to fashion our hearts into His image. This will speak before the Lord. We can also present our supplication before the Lord. Our persistent prayer from a heart bound to something that will not let go. This also will speak before the Lord. We also can come with thanksgiving and even receive communion that would testify before the Lord of our love, honor, and worship of who He is.

Receiving communion can speak before the Lord that we believe in Him and what He has done. On the basis of this, we can make our request. We can cry out to the Lord and ask that decisions would be rendered to deliver us from any and all crises. We can be granted such peace in our hearts that we might render judgments against the powers of satan from that peace and see him crushed under our feet. All of this can happen from the Courts of Heaven.

In the midst of this, we are absolutely dependent on the Holy Spirit and His help. Romans 8:26 tells us that when we don't know how or what to pray for as we ought, the Holy Spirit will guide us.

> *Likewise the Spirit also helps in our weaknesses. For we do not know what we should pray for as we ought, but*

the Spirit Himself makes intercession for us with groanings which cannot be uttered.

In the midst of any principles discussed, it is the Holy Spirit and His unction that will empower us. He has to show us how to employ and administer the principles we know. This can result in an ending of crisis and a reestablishing of peace.

There is one more thing I would mention in dealing with crisis in the Courts of Heaven. When Peter and John were arrested, harassed, and threatened by the religious authorities after the healing of the lame man, they and their company lifted a prayer to God. They did this from a place of fear and crisis. Acts 4:29-30 shows a part of their prayer that they offered to the Lord.

Now, Lord, look on their threats, and grant to Your servants that with all boldness they may speak Your word, by stretching out Your hand to heal, and that signs and wonders may be done through the name of Your holy Servant Jesus.

They presented the *threats* as evidence before the Lord. They then made their request for signs, wonders, and miracles and the faith to speak boldly. In the midst of crisis, it can be proper to present before the Lord what is scaring and even terrifying us. We can say, *"Lord, they are seeking to stifle us and remove faith from our hearts. Lord, behold their fear tactics."* This is heard before the Lord. You are saying, *"This is what the devil is doing. Let judgment come upon this thing."* As they prayed, the Bible says

God answered. Acts 4:31 says God shook the place and filled them.

> *And when they had prayed, the place where they were assembled together was shaken; and they were all filled with the Holy Spirit, and they spoke the word of God with boldness.*

There would be more persecution. However, the crisis of it would not affect them. God had heard their cry and answered with a verdict on their behalf. They would demonstrate the power, glory, boldness, and strength of God in the midst of anything that would touch them. No crisis would be a match to who the risen Lord was in them. They would demonstrate the Kingdom of God. They would give hope to the hopeless, help to the helpless, and power to those who were without might. A decision had been rendered from the Court of Heaven, and they would never be the same again.

ABOUT THE AUTHOR

Robert Henderson is a global apostolic leader who operates in revelation and impartation. His teaching empowers the body of Christ to see the hidden truths of Scripture clearly and apply them for breakthrough results. Driven by a mandate to disciple nations through writing and speaking, Robert travels extensively around the globe, teaching on the apostolic, the Kingdom of God, the "Seven Mountains" and most notably, the Courts of Heaven. He has been married to Mary for 40 years.

They have six children and five grandchildren. Together they are enjoying life in beautiful Waco, TX.

Made in the USA
Las Vegas, NV
26 November 2023